Interior Design Decades: 1920s-1940s Coloring Book

Greetings!

Welcome to the first book in a series of adult greyscale interior design coloring books, of epic interior design proportions! I am Sandeen, your coloring book artist/author and I currently live in Pittsburgh, PA with my wonderful husband, David. I come from a family of creative souls, including a few artists on both sides of my family. I earned my BFA in 2005, however, never really used my degree to its full potential. After realizing that I wound up buying way too many colorings books to count, I have decided that it wouldn't hurt to actually create my own for other fellow citizens of the world that love to color and let their inner creativity shine.

In this first book of the series, entitled, **Interior Design Decades: 1920s-1940s**, I take you back in time to what it would have been like to live in the 1920s, 1930s, and 1940s. This book features several designs of living room styles and kitchen styles that you would find during these time periods.

Upcoming greyscale coloring book in the next month will include interior designs of the 1950s-1970s. If you're a fan of interior design and enjoyed this book so far, the next upcoming book will be one that you should enjoy as well. I hope these books make you smile, help you to relieve stress, and allow you to share your artwork with your loved ones. When coloring, please feel free to use any coloring mediums you would like to help show off your creative talents.

Should you be interested to see what the original artwork looks like, you can find it on my Facebook page: https://www.facebook.com/royallycolorful. Additionally, all of the artwork is available to purchase on Redbubble (https://www.redbubble.com/people/RoyallyColorful/shop?asc=u) and on Fine Art America (https://www.fineartamerica.com/profiles/sandeen-scottoturner).

Thank you so much for purchasing this coloring book. Please don't forget to leave a review on amazon.com and share with others as this will support me in helping to create more amazing coloring books to come!

Until the next coloring book, Sandeen

<u>Fun Facts About The 1920s</u>

Here are some fun facts about the 1920s pulled from the U.S. Census website.

1. On August 18, 1920, the 19th Amendment to the U.S. Constitution is ratified prohibiting any U.S. citizens from being denied the right to vote based on sex.
2. KDKA in Pittsburgh, PA, becomes the first radio station to offer regular broadcasts on November 2, 1920.
3. On March 4, 1921, Congress approved the burial of an unidentified American soldier from World War I in the Tomb of the Unknown Soldier at Arlington National Cemetery.
4. Lila Bell and DeWitt Wallace begin publishing *Reader's Digest* in 1922.
5. F. Scott Fitzgerald publishes *The Great Gatsby* in 1925.

More information can be found at:
https://www.census.gov/history/www/through_the_decades/fast_facts/1920_fast_f
acts.html

Information About 1920s Interior Designs

This information provides a general overview about the interior design concepts of the 1920s pulled from Houzz.

The 1920s was known as The Roaring 20s. During this time, the use of Art Deco, Egyptian print motifs and Bauhaus designs were incorporated into everyday living rooms, kitchens, bedrooms, bathrooms, etc. Listed below are some of the designs that may have been present in these humble abodes.

***Ruhlmann Furniture**

***Lalique Glass**

***Brandt Metalwork**

***Skyscraper Furniture**

***Dunand Lacquerware**

***First Bauhaus House (Architecture)**

***Frankfurt Kitchen**

***Wassily Chair**

***Cesca Chair**

***Barcelona Chair**

***Bauhaus Lamp**

For more information regarding these designs and additional designs of the 1920s, please check out the following website: https://www.houzz.com/magazine/design-through-the-decades-the-1920s-stsetivw-vs-~118852929

1920s Living Room Designs

1920s Kitchen Designs

The 1930s Interior Designs

Fun Facts About The 1930s

Here are some fun facts about the 1930s pulled from the U.S. Census website.

1. 3M employee Richard Drew invents Scotch Brand Cellulose Tape in 1930. Today, it is widely known simply as "Scotch Tape."
2. The Mickey Mouse comic strip debuts in the January 13, 1930, edition of the *New York Mirror*.
3. On October 17, 1931, Chicago gangster Al Capone was convicted of Income Tax evasion and later sentenced to 11 years in federal prison.
4. Democrat Franklin D. Roosevelt defeats incumbent Republican Herbert Hoover in the 1932 election.
5. The Boulder Dam (today known as "Hoover Dam") is completed 2 years ahead of schedule on March 1, 1936.

More information can be found at:
https://www.census.gov/history/www/through_the_decades/fast_facts/1930_fast_f
acts.html

Information About 1930s Interior Designs

This information provides a general overview about the interior design concepts of the 1930s pulled from Houzz.

The 1930s was known as The Great Depression era. During this time, the use of transportation designs, naval designs and Oriental designs were incorporated into everyday living rooms, kitchens, bedrooms, bathrooms, etc. Listed below are some of the designs that may have been present in these humble abodes.

***SS Normandie Luxury**

***Orient Express Elegance**

***Dorn Textiles**

***Streamlining (also used in Architecture)**

***Fiesta Dinnerware**

***Depression Glass**

***Moka Express Coffee Pot**

***Anglepoise Lamp**

***Marais A Chair (a.k.a. Tolix Chair)**

***Tank Chair and Stacking Stool**

***Savoy Vase**

For more information regarding these designs and additional designs of the 1930s, please check out the following website: https://www.houzz.com/magazine/design-through-the-decades-the-1930s-stsetivw-vs-~119819223

1930s Living Room Designs

1930s Kitchen Designs

1940s Interior Designs

<u>**Fun Facts About The 1940s**</u>

Here are some fun facts about the 1940s pulled from the U.S. Census website.

1. Marvel Comics introduces superhero Captain America in March 1941.
2. After approximately 14 years, carving at Mount Rushmore concludes in October 1941.
3. Diarist Anne Frank and her family go into hiding in the "Acherhuis" on July 6, 1942, in Amsterdam.
4. Walt Disney wins a 1943 Academy Award for his animated short film *Der Fuehrer's Face*.
5. Band leader Alton Glenn Miller disappears while enroute to Paris, France, December 15, 1944.

More information can be found at:
https://www.census.gov/history/www/through_the_decades/fast_facts/1940_fast_facts.html

Information About 1940s Interior Designs

This information provides a general overview about the interior design concepts of the 1940s pulled from Houzz.

The 1940s were known as The War Years. During this time, the use of storage concepts, family room designs, and the start of mid-century designs were incorporated into everyday living rooms, kitchens, bedrooms, bathrooms, etc. Listed below are some of the designs that may have been present in these humble abodes.

***Nelson Ideas and Furnishings**

***Storage Walls**

***The Room Without A Name (a.k.a. Family Room/Den)**

***Platform Bench**

***Ball Clock**

***Noguchi Table**

***Molded Fiberglass Chairs**

***Case Study House No. 8 (Architecture)**

***Womb Chair**

***1006 Chair (a.k.a. Navy Chair)**

***Williams Architecture**

For more information regarding these designs and additional designs of the 1940s, please check out the following website: https://www.houzz.com/magazine/design-through-the-decades-the-1940s-stsetivw-vs-~120825134

1940s Living Room Designs

1940s Kitchen Designs